HAL LEONARD PIANO LIBRARY

BAROQUE TO MODERN

Intermediate Level

28 Pieces by 22 Composers in Progressive Order

Compiled and Edited by Richard Walters

On the cover:
Detail from *A Young Woman Composing Music* (c. 1662–63)
by Gabriël Metsu (1629–1667)

Detail from *Zíngaras* (1919)
by Rafael Barradas (1890–1929)

ISBN 978-1-4950-8862-9

G. SCHIRMER, *Inc.*

Distributed By

7777 W. Bluemound Rd. P.O. Box 13819 Milwaukee, WI 53213

www.musicsalesclassical.com
www.halleonard.com

CONTENTS

Though the table of contents appears in alphabetical order
by composer, the music in this book is in progressive order.

iv **COMPOSER BIOGRAPHIES, HISTORICAL NOTES and PRACTICE AND PERFORMANCE TIPS**

George Antheil
26 Little Shimmy

Carl Philipp Emanuel Bach
43 Solfeggietto in C minor, H. 220

Johann Sebastian Bach
48 Prelude in D minor, BWV 926
40 Prelude in C minor, BWV 999

Samuel Barber
34 Petite Berceuse
32 To My Steinway from *Three Sketches for Pianoforte*

Amy Marcy Beach
4 Gavotte in D minor from *Children's Album*, Op. 36, No. 2

Ludwig van Beethoven
8 German Dance in C Major, WoO 8, No. 7

Mélanie Bonis
46 Frère Jacques from *Scènes enfantines*, Op. 92, No. 6

Johann Friedrich Burgmüller
14 Restlessness (Inquiétude) from *25 Easy and Progressive Studies*, Op. 100, No. 18

Frédéric Chopin
33 Prelude in A Major, Op. 28, No. 7

Paul Creston
30 Rustic Dance from *Five Little Dances*, Op. 24, No. 1

George Frideric Handel
12 Prelude in G Major from *Suites de pièces*, Volume 2, HWV 442, No. 9

Stephen Heller
18 Study in A minor ("The Avalanche") from *25 Melodious Etudes*, Op. 45, No. 2

Dmitri Kabalevsky
Selections from *30 Pieces for Children*, Op. 27
28 Lyric Piece (No. 16)
20 The Chase (No. 21)

54 Rondo-Toccata from *Four Rondos*, Op. 60, No. 4

Aram Khachaturian
6 Andantino from *Children's Album*, Book 1

Edward Macdowell
10 To a Wild Rose from *Woodland Sketches*, Op. 51, No. 1

Wolfgang Amadeus Mozart
16 Adagio for Glass Harmonica, K. 356 (617a)
3 Funeral March for Signor Maestro Contrapunto, K. 453a

Robert Muczynski
50 Fable No. 9 from *Fables*, Op. 21, No. 9

Sergei Prokofiev
Selections from *Music for Children*, Op. 65
36 Morning (No. 1)
52 Promenade (No. 2)

Maurice Ravel
38 Prélude

Domenico Scarlatti
2 Sonata in D minor, L. 423 (K. 32, P. 14)

Robert Schumann
22 Of Strange Lands and People (Von fremden Ländern und Menschen) from *Scenes from Childhood* (*Kinderszenen*), Op. 15, No. 1

Dmitri Shostakovich
23 Birthday from *Children's Notebook for Piano*, Op. 69, No. 7

COMPOSER BIOGRAPHIES, HISTORICAL NOTES AND PRACTICE AND PERFORMANCE TIPS

GEORGE ANTHEIL
(1900–1959, American)

After studying with Constantin von Sternberg in Philadelphia and Ernest Bloch in New York, American composer George Antheil moved to Berlin in 1922. He travelled around Europe as a concert pianist, often performing his own works. In 1923 he moved to Paris, where he became a prominent member of the avant-garde, befriending James Joyce, Ezra Pound, W.B. Yeats, Erik Satie and Pablo Picasso. His most famous piece is *Ballet méchanique* (1925), scored for multiple pianos, player pianos, percussion, siren, and two propellers. Due to the practical performance issues, it is known more theoretically than for actual performance. Antheil's earlier works were often jazz-inspired, experimental and jarringly mechanistic. In the 1940s, back in the United States, Antheil turned to a more conventional style. A virtuoso concert pianist, he composed more for piano than any other instrument.

Little Shimmy
"Little Shimmy" was composed in 1923, the same year as Antheil's professional debut as a concert pianist (at the Théâtre des Champs-Elysées in Paris), and Antheil may have played it on this recital, a great success attended by his illustrious supporters, such as James Joyce, Erik Satie, Ezra Pound, Jean Cocteau and Darius Milhaud. Classical composers in the U.S., as well as in Paris and Berlin, were discovering American jazz and blues in this period and incorporating those sounds into compositions.

Practice and Performance Tips
- Antheil indicated neither tempo nor dynamics. Editorial suggestions are in brackets.
- The dotted eighth-note/sixteenth-note combination is like a "swing" beat.
- Note that the deliberately insistent and shrill high treble diads in measures 12 and 14 are straight eighth notes, not swing beat.
- This fun piece relies on a relentlessly steady rhythm in the left hand.
- The following tricky measures require special practice: 3, 11, 13, 15, and 21.
- Probably use no sustaining pedal.

CARL PHILIPP EMANUEL BACH
(1714–1788, German)

Carl Philipp Emanuel Bach, second son of Johann Sebastian Bach, was a major composer bridging the distinctions between late Baroque and early Classical periods, writing in the *empfindsamer Stil* (sensitive style), meaning an emotionally turbulent or dynamically expressive compositional style, as distinguished from the more restrained Rococo musical style. Carl received music lessons from his father until he began studies in law at Leipzig University and continued in Frankfurt. After graduation, C.P.E. Bach accepted a position in the court orchestra of Crown Prince Frederick of Prussia and moved to Berlin. In 1768 C.P.E. Bach became the music director of sacred music for the city of Hamburg, a position previously held by his godfather, Georg Philipp Telemann. C.P.E. Bach was extraordinarily prolific, writing over 1,000 works for voices and keyboard instruments.

Solfeggietto in C minor, H. 220

C.P.E Bach generally wrote in the more "modern" *stile galante*, not the contrapuntal high Baroque style of his famous father Johann Sebastian Bach. However, in this solfeggietto,composed in 1766, he harkens back to the earlier Baroque style. Most of the piece has a single note sounding at a time, with running sixteenth notes that outline harmonic movement. The implied harmony generally changes every two beats, on beats 1 and 3. For dramatic effect, at the climax of the piece (measures 21–24) the composer stops changing the harmony every two beats and instead sustains the harmony through the entire measure.

Practice and Performance Tips

- The technical challenge is to pass the sixteenth notes from hand to hand and maintain absolute evenness in touch and rhythm.
- Begin practice hands together, slowly.
- It would probably benefit most to divide the piece into sections for practice. Section 1: measures 1–12; section 2: measures 13–16; section 3: measures 17–25; section 4: measures 26–30; section 5: 31–35.
- Though a valid approach would be to use no pedal throughout the entire piece, some pianists may wish to experiment with light pedal, with the half notes and the whole notes in the bass line as a signal for pedaling.

JOHANN SEBASTIAN BACH

(1685–1750, German)

One of the greatest composers in the history of music, J. S. Bach defined the high Baroque style, developing counterpoint in composition further than any composer before him or since. However, during his lifetime he was more known for his virtuoso organ and harpsichord playing than for composition. Relatively few people were familiar with the works of J.S. Bach in the decades after his death. The modern wide recognition of Bach as a master composer began in the mid-nineteenth century, decades after his death, first championed by Felix Mendelssohn. Throughout his life Bach wrote keyboard music for his students, including his children. Bach composed hundreds of works, most for practical occasions, including cantatas, oratorios, motets, various instrumental suites, harpsichord works, organ works, and orchestral pieces. He came from a long line of musicians, and was father to six noted composers.

Prelude in D minor, BWV 926

Practice and Performance Tips

- Bach gave us no tempo marking for this piece. However, there is a clue as to what your individual tempo should be. Look at the fast moving sixteenth notes in measures 39–42. The performance tempo at which you ultimately arrive is determined by how well you can master these measures.
- This edition includes Bach's original few markings regarding articulation, notably the legato slurs in measures 9–10 and 13–14. Other than this, Bach gave us no articulation.
- Performance practice during the period would have taken care of other articulation expected in the piece. Stylistic suggestions have been made.
- The quarter notes which appear in the left hand in measures 10, 14, and 20–38 should be played with slight separation. Likewise, the moving eighth notes in the right hand, except when marked by Bach with slurs as legato, should also be played with a slight separation.
- The mordent which appears on the downbeat of measure 1 in the left hand may be played either beginning on the beat, or beginning slightly before the beat. In a slower tempo, a mordent such as this would always begin on the beat.

Prelude in C minor, BWV 999

(composed c. 1720)

Practice and Performance Tips

- Begin practice hands together, slowly.
- This piece uses the same rhythmic structure throughout except in the last two measures. The harmonic movement is the propelling factor in this piece, with the harmony changing for each measure.
- The sixteenth notes must be very evenly played. Play the left-hand eighth notes throughout slightly detached, with a bit of bounce.
- Editorial suggestions regarding dynamics appear in brackets.
- To help memorize it, you can play all of the notes in any measure together as a chord.
- Do not use sustaining pedal in this piece.
- There should be calmness in performance even though the music is quite busy.

SAMUEL BARBER

(1910–1981, American)

Born in Pennsylvania, Samuel Barber was a precocious musical talent who composed from an early age, and at fourteen began studies in singing, piano, and composition at the Curtis Institute. One of the most prominent American composers of the twentieth century, he is remembered for his distinctive neo-Romantic style. Early in his career he performed as a singer, which may have helped him develop an aptitude for writing the lyrical melodies that define his works. Barber wrote for orchestra, voice, choir, piano, chamber ensemble, and solo instruments and was acclaimed during his lifetime. After 1938, almost all of his compositions were written on commission from renowned performers and ensembles. Among his well-known pieces are the *Adagio for Strings* (1936), the opera *Vanessa* (1956–57), *Knoxville: Summer of 1915* (1947), and *Hermit Songs* (1953). Both "Petite Berceuse" and "To My Steinway" were composed in 1923, when Barber was thirteen. These were not published until 2010.

Petite Berceuse

Practice and Performance Tips

- Barber's music in general, including this piece, is about a strong sense of melodic phrase. The melody is in the right hand, the accompaniment is in the left hand.
- Practice hands separately at first. Aim for smoothness and expression in the right hand.
- Note the wide variety of dynamic markings, and use them expressively.
- There is some *rubato* (slight relaxing or surging of tempo) implied in this romantic piece, although the composer has written most of this in (measures 8–9, 15–17, 26–32). However, keep it simple (*dolce semplice*).
- Note the editorial suggestions for pedaling.
- Carefully practice measure 15, paying close notice to fingering.

To My Steinway
from *Three Sketches for Pianoforte*

Practice and Performance Tips

- This is a love song to the piano, with the top note of the right hand playing the melody.
- Play with a warm tone, and expressively.
- Context determines how fast or slow a chord should be rolled. In this adagio piece, the chords should not be rolled too quickly. Think of them as beautiful harmonies to be savored, emerging from the lowest note to the top note.
- Note the dramatic changes in dynamic from measures 5 to 8.
- The final arpeggio in measure 15 may be played freely, out of tempo.

AMY MARCY BEACH

(1867–1944, American)

Amy Beach (her maiden name was Amy Cheney) was one of the first female composers to be recognized with success in the United States. She composed her first piano piece at age four. Her first published piece came at age sixteen. That same year she made a debut as a pianist with the Boston Symphony. Her many works include the *Gaelic Symphony*, a piano concerto, the opera *Cabildo*, many piano pieces, chamber music, and over 150 art songs. Beach was deeply interested in theory and composition, and translated various treatises from French and German. In 1892 she became the first female composer to have a piece performed by the New York Symphony. After the death of her husband in 1910, she composed and performed for the rest of her life, and was a leading cultural figure of her day. Beach had the condition of synesthesia, a neurological association of color with sound.

Gavotte in D minor
from *Children's Album*, Op. 36, No. 2

This is one of five pieces in *Children's Album*, composed in 1897. A gavotte was a dance movement in the Baroque Era. Composers after the Baroque period used the label "gavotte" vaguely, and virtually none of the Baroque characteristics were retained. Beach probably meant a light dancelike quality for this piece in giving it this title.

Practice and Performance Tips

- Begin practice slowly, hands separately.
- Divide the piece into natural sections for practice. Section 1: measures 1–8; section 2: measures 9–16; section 3: measures 17–24; section 4: measures 25–40; section 7: measures 41–56.
- The music asks for a precise, light tough.
- Beach's articulation markings are very specific. Pay attention!
- Make the most of the drastic changes of dynamics.
- The spots marked *sopra* in measures 23 and 38 mean that the right hand crosses the left hand, but just barely.
- A good test of your *allegro* tempo is how gracefully you can play measures 11–12.

LUDWIG VAN BEETHOVEN

(1770–1827, German)

Beethoven was the major figure of the transition from the Classical Era to the Romantic Era in music. As one of the first successful freelance composers, as opposed to a composer thriving in a royal court appointment, Beethoven wrote widely in nearly every genre of his day, with emphasis on instrumental music. He acquired wealth and fame beyond any composer before him. Beethoven's chamber music, piano sonatas, concertos, and symphonies are part of the ever-present international repertoire. In his youth he was regarded as one of the greatest pianists of his time, but he stopped performing after hearing loss set in. He devoted an enormous amount of his compositional efforts to the piano, which as an instrument came of age during his lifetime. He was occasionally a piano teacher, with wealthy patrons and young prodigies begging for lessons, though this task was not a match for his nature. However, teaching piano did inspire him to write many pieces for students. Because his piano music is so widely spread across the level of difficulty from easy to virtuosic, Beethoven's piano music is played by students and professional pianists. .

German Dance in C Major, WoO 8, No. 7
This "German Dance" was composed in 1795.

Practice and Performance Tips

- The first section (measures 1–17) features the right hand in continuous eighth notes. Practice the right hand alone.
- Aim for evenness and a flow in the moving eighth notes in the first section.
- Notice the long phrase over the right hand from measure 1–7.
- In contrast to the smooth, phrased motion of the right hand in measures 8–17, the left hand plays crisp *staccato* chords.
- Note the sharp and sudden changes in dynamics, from ***p*** to ***f*** and back to ***p***.
- Tempo is open to interpretation since Beethoven provided no indication. An acceptable tempo might range from quarter note = 130 to 168.
- Common to the period, do not play the repeats in the *da capo* of the first section.

MÉLANIE BONIS
(1858–1937, French)

Because woman were not taken seriously as composers in the 19th century, Mélanie Bonis used the male pen name Mel Bonis. Though she showed extraordinary talent, her working class Parisian family was opposed to her musical study. César Franck taught her as a teenager and through him she enrolled in the Paris Conservatoire, studying piano, harmony and composition, and winning prizes. Her parents were against her romance with a singer, and forced her to marry a well-off man 25 years older than she. Her husband and children showed no interest in her music. In the 1890s she had an affair with the singer she had fallen in love with at the Conservatoire years before, and secretly had an illegitimate child she could not acknowledge for many years. Bonis became a member of the French composer's society, including being recognized as a remarkable talent by elite composers of the day, such as Saint-Saëns. In the first decade of the 20th century, her music had some public performances. She suffered from poor health in her last years, but continued composing. Bonis was extraordinarily driven as a composer, writing on her own without hearing her music. She wrote over 300 works of chamber music, art song, choral music, orchestral pieces, and piano music. Only a few compositions were published in her lifetime, and included *Scènes enfantines* (*Scenes of Childhood*), Op. 92, composed in 1912.

Frère Jacques
from *Scènes enfantines*, Op. 92, No. 6

Practice and Performance Tips

- The piece is built on the familiar song "Frère Jacques" ("Are You Sleeping, Brother John" in English).
- The fun is hearing that simple melody treated in different settings throughout.
- Practice slowly hands separately. This piece requires a strong independence of the hands.
- Bonis has carefully composed specific articulation for every note or group of notes.
- The strongly accented notes, such as in measures 1–4, should by implication be played slightly detached.
- Make certain you play the accents, the *staccatos*, and the phrase-slurred notes distinctly differently.
- *trés court* over the barline between measures 40 and 41 means a short pause before going on.
- The commas after measures 41, 42 and 43 might symbolize nodding off.
- By the quiet ending we can assume the brother has fallen asleep.
- Only use sustaining pedal where Bonis has composed it.

JOHANN FRIEDRICH BURGMÜLLER
(1806–1874, German/French)

The Burgmüllers were a musical family. Johann August Franz, the patriarch, was a composer and theatre music director as well as the founder of the Lower Rhine Music Festival. Johann Friedrich's brother Norbert was a child prodigy at the piano and a composer. Johann Freidrich distinguished himself from his family by leaving Germany and establishing a career in Parisian circles as a composer of French salon music. Later in life he withdrew from performing and focused on teaching. He wrote many short character pieces for his students as etudes. Several collections of these are perennial favorites of piano teachers, especially opuses 100, 105, and 109.

Restlessness (Inquiétude) from *25 Easy and Progressive Studies*, Op. 100, No. 18

Practice and Performance Tips

- The simple elements are *staccato* chords in the left hand answered by three slurred sixteenth notes in the right hand.
- Practice the insistent left-hand staccato chords separately, keeping them even and crisp.
- Then practice slowly, hands together, marking the contrast between the *staccato* left hand and the slurred notes in the right hand.
- The piece divides easily into practice sections. Section 1: measures 1–8; section 2: measures 9–16; section 3: measures 17–24; section 4: the second ending to the end.
- Gradually increase practice speed, but always maintain a steady tempo.
- As with all his jewel-like pieces, Burgmüller has composed contrasting dynamics throughout that need to be carefully observed.
- Notice the *subito* ***f*** under the second ending in measure 25; the texture of the left hand changes here as the composer asks the pianist to slur rather than play *staccato*.

FRÉDÉRIC CHOPIN

(1810–1849, Polish/French)

A major Romantic era composer for piano, Chopin created a uniquely personal, forward-thinking style, and revolutionized literature for the instrument. He left his native Poland at age 20 after an education at the Warsaw Conservatory, first briefly to Vienna before settling in Paris for most of the remainder of his life. Chopin became a much sought after piano teacher in the French capital, and was part of the lively salon culture, where he preferred to perform instead of in large concert halls. He is reputed to have had an extremely refined, poetic touch as a pianist. He was in chronic frail health through much of his adult life, and died at the young age of 39, probably brought on by tuberculosis. Because of political upheaval, Chopin was never able to return to Poland, and his nostalgic ache for his homeland is a characteristic heard in his music. The preludes were composed 1836–39.

Prelude in A Major, Op. 28, No. 7

Practice and Performance Tips

- Practice hands separately, until you can play each hand gracefully.
- This prelude is as if a graceful waltz has been put under a microscope, slowed down and contemplated at leisure. It is almost like a wistful, nostalgic memory.
- The volume increases only at the point of the surprising change of harmony on the downbeat of measure 12.
- Note that the pedal clears for the quarter-note pickup that begins the next phrase.
- It would be a great mistake to play this music too quickly.

PAUL CRESTON

(1906–1985, American)

Paul Creston was born into a poor Italian immigrant family in New York. As a child he took piano and organ lessons but was self-taught in theory and composition. In 1938 Creston was awarded a Guggenheim Fellowship, and in 1941 the New York Music Critics' Circle Award. He served as the director of A.S.C.A.P. from 1960–1968, and was composer-in-residence and professor of music at Central Washington State College from 1968–1975. His works, which include orchestral, vocal, piano, and chamber music repertoire, often feature shifting rhythmic patterns. He wrote a number of solos for instruments customarily left out of the limelight, such as the marimba, accordion, or saxophone. Creston was an important composition teacher (John Corigliano studied with him), and also wrote the books *Principles of Rhythm and Rational Metric Notation*.

Rustic Dance
from *Five Little Dances*, Op. 24, No. 1

The *Five Little Dances* were composed in 1940.

Practice and Performance Tips

- Begin practice slowly hands separately.
- Learn the articulations (accents, staccato) as you learn the notes and rhythms.
- Divide the piece into sections for your practice. For instance: Section 1: measures 1–12; Section 2: measures 13–24; Section 3: measures 25–34; Section 4: measures 35–46.

- Notice how the texture changes from accented, loud and *non legato* to smooth and soft in measure 13.
- When you can play each hand separately accurately, move to practicing hands together at a slow tempo.
- Continue to observe the articulations you learned when practicing hands separately.
- Pay careful attention to the dynamics the composer has written.
- Do not take this piece too quickly as a performance tempo.
- Keep the tempo absolutely steady.
- Note the composer's marking "Heavily" and the title "Rustic Dance" in finding the character of the music.

GEORGE FRIDERIC HANDEL

(1685–1759, German/British)

Handel was one of the defining composers of the Baroque period. After a brief time in Italy as a young man, he spent nearly his entire adult career in London, where he became famous as a composer of opera and oratorio, including *Messiah*, now his most recognizable music. Handel also wrote numerous concertos, suites, overtures, cantatas, trio sonatas, and solo keyboard works. Though he taught some students early in his career and occasionally instructed members of the London aristocracy, Handel was not known for his teaching abilities. His keyboard works were likely not written for any of his students, but to fulfill commissions or generate income from publication. Handel composed various keyboard works until 1720, then he became master of the orchestra for the Royal Academy of Music, an organization dedicated to performing new operas. After Italian opera fell out of fashion in London, Handel turned his compositional efforts to oratorio.

Prelude in G Major from *Suites de pièces*, Volume 2, HWV 442, No. 9
The *Suites de pièces* was composed c. 1703–06.

Practice and Performance Tips

- Practice hands separately and slowly at first.
- Articulation and steadiness are the key factors in this prelude.
- We have suggested that some eighth notes be played *staccato*, and some in two-note slurs, which will create appropriate style.
- The quarter notes should be played slightly detached.
- At an *allegro* tempo, the sixteenth notes by default will be played slurred.
- The touch should be light, refined, and elegant, and the mood joyous.
- Use no sustaining pedal.

STEPHEN HELLER

(1813–1888, Hungarian/French)

Heller begged his parents for piano lessons as a child. At the age of seven he was already writing music for a small band put together by his father. The boy was sent to Vienna to study with Carl Czerny, but quickly found the lessons too expensive and instead studied with Anton Halm, who introduced Heller to Beethoven and Schubert. At age 13 Heller was giving concerts in Vienna as a pianist and two years later began touring Europe. His travels brought him in contact with Chopin, Liszt, Paganini, and most importantly Robert Schumann, with whom he developed a life-long friendship. Heller even contributed to Schumann's journal *Neue Zeitschrift* under the pseudonym Jeanquirit. After two years of touring, the rigorous schedule became too much for the boy and Heller settled first in Ausburg, and then in Paris to teach and compose. He wrote several hundred piano pieces, of which the short character pieces from opuses 45, 46, and 47 are frequently performed today.

Study in A minor ("The Avalanche") from *25 Melodious Etudes*, Op. 45, No. 2
Heller composed *25 Melodious Etudes* in 1844. The nickname "The Avalanche" does not appear in the first edition, but somehow the piece has become known by that name. The "avalanche" does not begin with downward movement, but upward movement. Perhaps Heller had in mind the frenzied running away from the sudden avalanche.

Practice and Performance Tips

- Practice slowly, hands together in sections. Section 1: measures 1–16; section 2: measures 17–32; section 3: measures 33–48; section 4: measures 49–72; section 5: measures 73–89.
- Even in the early stages of slow practice, explicitly apply the articulation Heller composed.
- Play the slurred *staccato* chords in 13–14 and 29–30 with separation; imagine them being notated as eighth-note chords followed by eighth-note rests.
- The tempo should relax just a bit in measures 13–16 and 29–32 at *poco meno mosso*.

- Make sure the triplets are evenly played throughout. A listener should not be able to tell that you move from hand to hand with them.
- Make the most of Heller's detailed dynamic markings. Note the sudden switch from ***mf*** to ***p*** in measures 13 and 29.
- It is recommended that you practice A minor scales as you work on this piece.
- Only use the sustaining pedal where indicated.

DMITRI KABALEVSKY

(1904–1987, Russian)

Kabalevsky was an important Russian composer of the Soviet era who wrote music in many genres, including four symphonies, a handful of operas, theatre and film scores, patriotic music, choral music, vocal music, and numerous piano works. He embraced the Soviet notion of socialist realism in art, a fact that was politically advantageous to his career in the USSR. While studying piano and composition at the Moscow Conservatory, he taught piano lessons at a music college and it was for these students that he began writing works for young players. In 1932 he started teaching at the Moscow Conservatory, earning the title of professor in 1939. He eventually went on to develop programs for the concert hall, radio, and television aimed at teaching children about classical music. In the last decades of his life, Kabalevsky focused on developing music curricula for schools, retiring from the Moscow Conservatory to teach in public schools where he could test his theories and the effectiveness of his syllabi. This he considered his true life's work, and his pedagogical principles revolutionized music education in Russia. A collection of his writings on music education was published in English in 1988 as *Music and Education: A Composer Writes About Musical Education.*

Selections from *30 Pieces for Children,* Op. 27

Kabalevsky often quoted Maxim Gorki, saying that books for children should be "the same as for adults, only better." Kabalevsky believed strongly in writing music for students that was not dumbed-down, but rather, complete, imaginative compositions unto themselves. The set was composed in 1937–38. Kabalevsky did a slight revision of Op. 27 in 1985, which was intended to be an authoritative edition. (This is our source for the pieces in this collection.)

Lyric Piece (No. 16)

Practice and Performance Tips

- As might be guessed of music titled "Lyric Piece," it is primarily about song-like melody.
- The right-hand melody should predominate over the left-hand accompaniment in measures 3–12.
- The melody moves to the left hand in measures 12–17, before returning to the right hand in measure 17.
- Practice the melody, noted above, separately, aiming to create a smooth and musically pleasing line, using the phrasing that Kabalevsky has composed to shape the melody.
- The melancholy spirit, combined with the long melody, is reminiscent of Chopin.
- Pedaling is explicitly marked by the composer.
- The composer takes the music into unexpected harmony in measure 17, then again in measure 21.
- Except for the opening motive, which returns at the end of measure 31, this is quiet music, marked ***p***. Do not allow it to bloom too far past that quiet dynamic. Practice the left hand alone with the pedaling.

The Chase (No. 21)

Practice and Performance Tips

- This piece, with hands in octaves throughout, creates a brilliant and exciting impact.
- When well played it sounds harder than it actually is, because the music lies so easily under the hands.
- Divide the piece into sections and practice slowly hands and separately.
- For instance practice measures 1–8 first with right hand only, then left hand only.
- Continue throughout the piece in sections with this approach.
- Left-hand agility is the challenge for most student pianists.
- When putting hands together, only play as quickly as the left hand has mastered the music.
- From the very beginning of practice pay attention to slurs, *staccato* and accents.
- Learning the articulation from the start will help you learn the notes and rhythms.
- Kabalevsky would have written in pedaling had he intended it. Use no pedal.

Rondo-Toccata from *Four Rondos,* Op. 60, No. 4

(composed 1958)

Practice and Performance Tips

- The piece can create a brilliant impact in performance. Because the left hand remains in a contained position through much of it, it will sound more difficult than it is.
- Practice hands separately, slowly at first.

- Learn the articulation (*staccato* touch) from the beginning.
- Use the sustaining pedal only where explicitly indicated by Kabalevsky.
- Note the change of touch, moving from *staccato* to *legato* in measure 17.
- With the hands playing the same notes in octaves beginning in measure 19, make sure both right and left hands are playing exactly the same articulation.
- Practice tempo can increase as you master the music, but always maintain steadiness.
- Only play the piece as fast as you can manage in making it sound under control. Do not let it run away from you.

ARAM KHACHATURIAN

(1903–1978, Soviet/Armenian)

Aram Khachaturian was a seminal figure in 20th century Armenian and Soviet culture. Beloved in his homeland for bringing Armenia to prominence within the realm of Western art music, a major concert hall in Armenia's capital Yerevan bears his name, as well as a string quartet and an international competition for piano and composition. Born in Tbilisi, Georgia, of Armenian heritage, he grew up listening to Armenian folk songs but was also exposed to classical music early on through the Tbilisi's chapter of the Russian Music Society, the city's Italian Opera Theater, and visits by musicians such as Sergei Rachmaninoff. He moved to Moscow to study composition in 1921. Khachaturian's musical language combined Armenian folk influences with the Russian romantic tradition, embodying the official Soviet arts policy. He used traditional forms, such as theme and variations, sonata form, and Baroque suite forms, in creative ways, juxtaposing them with Armenian melodies and religious songs, folk dance rhythms, and a harmonic language that took inspiration from folk instruments such as the saz. He wrote symphonies, instrumental concertos, sonatas, ballets, and was the first Armenian composer to write film music. Khachaturian's most recognizable composition to the general public is "Sabre Dance" from the ballet *Gayane*. Starting in 1950, he also became active as an internationally touring conductor. He was awarded the Order of Lenin in 1939 and the Hero of Socialist Labor in 1973.

Andantino from *Children's Album,* Book 1
(composition begun 1926, completed 1947)
Khachaturian composed two *Albums for Children.* The first, completed in 1947, included *Adventures of Ivan.*

Practice and Performance Tips
- The right hand is the singing (*cantabile*), rather sad melody throughout; the left hand is an accompaniment to this melody.
- Practice the right-hand melody separately, making it expressive in the way the composer intends, using the dynamics, *crescendos*, *decrescendos*, and slurs.
- The left hand also needs practice separately.
- Play the repeated quarter note diads in the left hand very evenly.
- Practice the pedaling Khachaturian has composed, applying it very specifically when practicing left hand alone.
- Except for the spot marked *rit.* (measures 16–17, the beat should be played steadily throughout.

EDWARD MACDOWELL

(1860–1908, American)

Edward MacDowell showed talent at the piano from an early age. At 16 his mother took him to France to study at the Conservatoire de Paris. He continued his studies in Germany, where he met and performed for Franz Liszt, who encouraged the young composer. MacDowell married and in 1888 returned to the United States, settling in Boston. In 1896, the year *Woodland Sketches* was composed, he became professor of composition at Columbia University in New York. MacDowell was fundamental in building the music program at the school. He retired in 1904 following a buggy accident that gradually reduced his mental and physical health until his death. The MacDowell Colony in Petersburg, New Hampshire, was established in his honor for artists to find inspiration and solitude. MacDowell is often cited as the first American composer to gain stature and success in the European dominated classical music of his era.

To a Wild Rose
from *Woodland Sketches,* Op. 51, No. 1
Practice and Performance Tips
- Practice hands separately.
- Practice can begin at a louder volume, such as ***mf***, while you become secure in the notes.
- Aim for smoothness and tenderness in the top note melody of the right hand.
- The piece is primarily soft, with variations in volume. Strive for an even sound with a rounded tone as you play softly.
- The music arrives at ***f*** only once, at measure 25, and right way the volume decreases.

- Practice without sustaining pedal, and try to play as legato as possible with the fingers only.
- After you have mastered the piece, then very carefully add sustaining pedal, changing the pedal with every change of harmony.

WOLFGANG AMADEUS MOZART
(1756–1791, Austrian)

One of the most astonishing talents in the history of music, Mozart was first a child prodigy as a composer, keyboard player and violinist. He developed into one of the greatest composers who has ever lived, with a vast output in opera, symphonies, choral music, keyboard music, and chamber music, all accomplished before his death at the young age of 35. Mozart spent most of his adult life living and working in Vienna. He was at the end of the era when successful musicians and composers attained substantial royal court appointments. A major position of this sort eluded him, despite his enormous talent, and he constantly sought opportunities to compose and perform. His music embodies the eighteenth century "age of reason" in its refined qualities, but adds playfulness, earnestness, sophistication and a deep sense of melody and harmony. Mozart's piano sonatas, concertos, sets of variations, and many other pieces at all levels from quite easy to virtuosic have become standards in the literature. His first compositions as a boy, from age five, were for keyboard.

Adagio for Glass Harmonica, K. 356 (617a)
"Adagio for Glass Harmonica" was written in 1791 for Marianne Krichgeßner, the nearly blind glass harmonica player who gave the first performance of a version for glass harmonica, flute, oboe, violin, and cello on August 19, 1791 in Vienna. The glass harmonica uses a series of glass bowls or goblets to produce musical tones through friction. The ethereal ringing sound produced is similar to when a finger rubs the moistened rim of a drinking glass.

Practice and Performance Tips
- Practice slowly hands separately, then hands together.
- When practicing, use no sustaining pedal.
- Aim for beautiful *legato* and evenness.
- Very carefully execute all details of articulation to achieve Mozartean style. Editorial suggestions in this edition will help find the appropriate style.
- Do not let this classical era piece become too romantic and exaggerated. Maintain restraint.

Funeral March for Signor Maestro Contrapunto, K. 453a
The comic "Funeral March for Signor Maestro Contrapunto" was composed in 1784 for a student.

Practice and Performance Tips
- Performing this march, which is very dramatic with many *subito* changes in dynamics, requires a solemn-faced seriousness similar to an actor playing a very serious (and ultimately very ironic) role in a comedy.
- Cleanly execute the sudden changes from ***f*** to ***p*** and back to ***f***.
- Don't overplay the ***f*** sections with too much volume.
- Practice the parallel sixths (measures 2 and 14) and thirds (measures 4, 11–12) slowly and carefully, attempting *legato* with the fingers.
- A limited amount of sustaining pedal is possible, suggested in brackets in this edition.

ROBERT MUCZYNSKI
(1929–2010, American)

Composer and pianist Robert Muczynski studied at DePaul University in his hometown of Chicago with Alexander Tcherepnin. A brilliant pianist, at twenty-nine he made his Carnegie Hall debut with a performance of his own compositions. In addition to solo piano works, Muczynski mainly wrote for small chamber ensembles and also composed several orchestral pieces. His flute and saxophone sonatas, as well as *Time Pieces* for clarinet and piano, have become part of the standard repertoire for those instruments. In 1981, his concerto for saxophone was nominated for the Pulitzer Prize. Muczynski was composer in residence on the faculty of the University of Arizona from 1965 until his retirement in 1988.

Fable No. 9 from *Fables*, Op. 21, No. 9
Fables, subtitled "Nine Pieces for the Young," was composed in 1965 for eight-year-old piano student.

Practice and Performance Tips
- Begin practice slowly hands separately, retaining a steady eighth note beat.
- You may divide your practice into three sections. Section 1: measures 1–8; Section 2: measures 9–18; Section 3: measures 19–29.
- In Sections 1 and 3 pay careful attention to the composer's accents, slurs and staccato markings in the right hand. These will help propel the insistent rhythm.

- In Sections 1 and 3 the left-hand eighth notes must be absolutely steady.
- Move to practicing hands together, first at a slow tempo, but retaining a steady beat.

SERGEI PROKOFIEV

(1891–1953, Russian)

Russian composer and pianist Sergei Prokofiev pushed the boundaries of Russian romanticism without fully disregarding its influence. Influenced by the formal aspects of works by Haydn and Mozart, he was also a pioneering neo-classicist. Prokofiev was born in eastern Ukraine, but travelled often with his mother to Moscow and St. Petersburg where he was exposed to works such as Gounod's *Faust*, Borodin's *Prince Igor*, Tchaikovsky's *Sleeping Beauty*, and operas such as *La Traviata* and *Carmen*. His prodigious musical abilities as a child led him to lessons with Reinhold Glière and then studies at the St. Petersburg Conservatory. He composed several sonatas and symphonies during his studies, as well as his first piano concerto, which he played for his piano exam at the conservatory, taking first prize. In 1917, following the October Revolution, he left Russia, first moving to the United States and then settling in Europe. He continued to tour internationally after returning to the Soviet Union in 1936, until the authorities confiscated his passport two years later. During World War II Prokofiev was evacuated from the USSR. It was a difficult time for composers and artists in Soviet Russia. Between 1946 and 1948, Soviet political leader Andrey Zhdanov passed a number of resolutions with the intent of heavily regulating artistic output and keeping it in line with the ideals of socialist realism and the Communist Party. In 1935, in the midst of many months of work on the large ballet *Romeo and Juliet*, a commission from the Kirov Ballet, Prokofiev refreshed his creativity briefly by shifting his focus to composing the twelve piano miniatures comprising *Music for Children*, Op. 65.

Morning from *Music for Children*, Op. 65, No. 1

Practice and Performance Tips

- One of the implied topics that Prokofiev is teaching is the need for a graceful shift of hand position into different ranges of the piano, including the crossing of hands. These need to be anticipated and played with elegance or they will sound clumsy.
- Divide the piece into sections for practice. Section 1: measures 1–8; Section 2: measures 9–17; Section 3: measures 18–23; Section 4: measures 24–29.
- Though the music is full of colorful features and figures, it is contained in volume and quiet in spirit.
- It may help some pianists to first learn the piece playing at ***mf***, then later apply the composer's dynamics of ***p***, ***mp***, ***pp***, etc.
- Practice measures 9–17 right hand alone, playing with evenness and clarity.
- Bring out the left-hand melody in measures 9–17, playing with beautiful tone and *legato* phrasing.
- The hands trade at measure 18, with the eighth notes moving to the left hand. Practice left hand alone in this section, aiming for evenness and clarity.
- Play measure 23 very gracefully or the notes will sound "wrong."
- Apply tasteful use of the sustaining pedal.

Promenade from *Music for Children*, Op. 65, No. 2

Practice and Performance Tips

- The composer's implication for the left-hand quarter notes in measures 1–20 without articulation markings is that these should be played with slight separation. If he had intended legato playing, he would have indicated this.
- The above means that in spots such as measures 4 or 6, the right hand is playing a smooth *legato* and the left hand is playing slightly detached.
- Practice without any sustaining pedal. The entire piece would easily be played with no pedal. If you choose to add it in spots, use taste and care.
- Anticipate the crossing of hands to manage it gracefully, in measures 45–50.
- Do not take this *Allegretto* too quickly.

MAURICE RAVEL

(1875–1937, French)

Ravel was born in Ciboure, a Basque villa in the southwestern corner of France to Swiss and Basque parents, but raised in Paris, his lifelong use of exotic influences in his music stemmed from his heritage-based affinity for Basque and Spanish culture. Ravel studied piano and then composition with Gabriel Fauré at the Paris Conservatoire, though he was dismissed for not meeting the necessary requirements in either piano or composition. This, along with his heritage, may have influenced the lack of support he received from French music critics and the Société Nationale de Musique, Paris' leading concert society. Critics often pitted him unfavorably against Debussy and accused him of copying Debussy's style. In 1909, Ravel founded the Société Musicale Indépendente in opposition to the Société Nationale, naming Fauré president. This society strove to organize performances of both French and foreign works regardless of their style or genre. The same year Ravel wrote *Daphnis et Chloé* for famed choreographer Diaghilev and began his close friendship with Igor Stravinsky. He joined the army as a driver in the motor transport corps during World War I, a tragic time in which he was also deeply affected by the loss of his mother, with whom he was extremely close. He lived the rest of his life thirty miles west of Paris in Montfortl'Amaury surrounded by the Forest of Rambouillet, travelling around Europe and North America performing and attending premieres of his works.

Prélude
This little known prelude was composed in 1913.

Practice and Performance Tips

- French style in the Impressionist period requires sophistication of touch, phrasing, pedaling and musicality.
- This piece is about elegant, languorous phrase and lush harmony.
- Play the eighth note figures throughout very smoothly.
- Pay careful attention to Ravel's phrase markings.
- The section measures 10–15 will require careful attention, as the hands are close together, with the right hand playing on top of the left hand.
- The rolled chord in the right hand in measure 16 and 18 will take some practice for most hands. If your hand is too small to hold all the notes down after they are rolled, then experiment with letting one or two of the notes go, sustaining the sound with careful use of the sustaining pedal.
- Pedal needs to be applied. Be careful to keep the harmonies clear. Do make this or any other Impressionist piece a vague blur of sound.

DOMENICO SCARLATTI
(1685–1757, Italian)

Domenico was one of two musical sons of composer Alessandro Scarlatti. Domenico was extraordinarily influential in the development of Italian solo keyboard music, composing nearly 600 sonatas for the instrument. He was taught by his father and other musicians in Naples until he secured the position of composer and organist for the royal chapel in Naples at the age of 15. He spent time in Venice and Rome serving as the Maestro di cappella at St. Peter's before moving to Lisbon, where he taught the Portuguese Princess. In 1728, he moved to Spain where he would spend the rest of his life, finally settling in Madrid, where he was the music master for the Princess and later Queen of Spain. A sonata in the Italian Baroque almost always meant a one-movement instrumental piece. Its musical form was not defined and could be many possibilities. The Italian Baroque style is distinctly different from the German Baroque style and the French Baroque style. Without going into complicated detail, the Italian Baroque style had more freedom than its German counterpart.

Sonata in D minor, L. 423 (K. 32, P. 14)
Practice and Performance Tips

- This aria, closely related to vocal music, has a typical quality of Baroque melancholy.
- The thirty-second notes which appear many places are written out ornaments in this edition.
- We have made stylistic suggestions about which notes should be slurred (meaning that the notes in the slurred group are played *legato*) and which should be played *staccato*.
- The short two-note and three-note slurs are a typical Baroque musical indication of weeping.
- Strive for evenness and expression; use no sustaining pedal.

ROBERT SCHUMANN
(1810–1856, German)

One of the principal composers of the Romantic era, Robert Schumann's relatively short creative career gave the world major repertoire in symphonies, art song, chamber music, and piano music. Besides being a composer, Schumann was an accomplished writer about music, especially as a critic, then editor of the influential *Neue Zeitschrift für Musik*. He was married to concert pianist Clara Wieck, who championed his works after his death, the result a severe struggle with mental illness. Schumann was an early supporter of the young Johannes Brahms. *Album for the Young* (*Album für die Jugend*), a collection of 43 short piano pieces, was composed in 1838 for Schumann's three daughters. Schumann made a specialty of short character pieces for piano, not entirely unrelated to his distinctive work as a major composer of art song.

Of Strange Lands and People
(Von fremden Ländern und Menschen)
from *Scenes from Childhood (Kinderszenen)*,
Op. 15, No. 1

One of Schumann's most famous piano pieces, the title "Of Strange Lands and People" implies dreamy imagination of places far away. It is from *Kinderszenen* (Scenes from Childhood), composed in 1838.

Practice and Performance Tips

- The music is constructed in three voices.
- The treble melody is the top note in the right hand. (This voice is supported by an alto harmony underneath it in measures 9–12.)
- The second voice is the bass line, single notes throughout, the lowest note in the writing.
- The third voice is that of the moving triplets.
- There also is an implied fourth voice, which is the first note of the triplet figure in measures 1–8 and measure 15 to the end.
- The composer apparently gave this piece no tempo marking. Too often, one hears a student pianist play this piece too quickly and too loudly, destroying its wistful dreaminess.
- Practice slowly, hands together without pedal, striving for *legato*.

DMITRI SHOSTAKOVICH

(1906–1975, Russian)

A major mid-20th century composer, Shostakovich is famous for his epic symphonies, concertos, operas, string quartets, and other chamber works. Born in St. Petersburg, his entire career took place in Soviet-era Russia. His life teetered between receiving high official honors and living with an almost debilitating fear of arrest for works that did not adhere to the Soviet ideals of socialist realism. In 1934, his opera *Lady Macbeth of the Mtsensk District* met with great popular success, but was banned by Stalin for the next thirty years as modernist, surrealist, and obscene. The following year, Stalin began a campaign known as the Purges, executing or exiling to prison camps politicians, intellectuals, and artists. Shostakovich managed to avoid such a fate, and despite an atmosphere of anxiety and repression, was able to compose an astounding number of works with originality, humor, and emotional power. He succeeded in striking a balance between modernism and tradition that continues to make his music accessible to a broad audience. An excellent pianist, Shostakovich performed concertos by Mozart, Prokofiev, and Tchaikovsky early in his career, but after 1930 limited himself to performing his own works and some chamber music. He taught instrumentation and composition at the Leningrad Conservatory from 1937–1968, with brief breaks due to war and other political disruptions, and at the Moscow Conservatory in the 1940s. Since his death in 1975, Shostakovich has become one of the most-performed 20th century composers.

Birthday from *Children's Notebook for Piano*,
Op. 69, No. 7

Children's Notebook for Piano was written for his eight-year-old daughter, Galina, for her studies on the instrument. The original set, composed in 1944, was published as six pieces. The seventh piece, "Birthday," written in celebration of Galina's ninth birthday in 1945, was added in a later edition.

Practice and Performance Tips

- The eighth-note triplet *staccato* chords in measures 1, 3, 5, and later in measures 48–50, should be played with a crisp, buoyant bounce. Keep your wrists relaxed and avoid tension.
- After the introduction "fanfare," the music settles into a rather languid waltz in measure 7.
- Practice hands separately, paying careful attention to the composer's slurs and *staccato* markings.
- Divide the piece into sections for practice. Section 1: measures 1-6; Section 2: measures 7–16; Section 3: measures 17–24; Section 4: measures 24–40; Section 4: measures 41–48; Section 5: measures 48–54.
- Do not forget the general festive spirit of celebration.

— Richard Walters, editor

These pieces were previously published in the following Schirmer Performance Editions volumes.

Antheil: Little Shimmy
Barber: Petite Berceuse
Barber: To My Steinway from *Three Sketches for Piano*
Creston: Rustic Dance from *Five Little Dances*, Op. 24, No. 1
Kabalevsky: Rondo-Toccata from *Four Rondos*, Op. 60, No. 4
Muczynski: Fable No. 9 from *Fables*, Op. 21, No. 9
Ravel: Prélude
from *The 20th Century: Intermediate Level*
edited by Richard Walters

C.P.E Bach: Solfeggietto in C minor, H. 220
from *The Classical Era: Intermediate Level*
edited by Richard Walters

Prelude in D minor, BWV 926
Prelude in C minor, BWV 999
from J.S. *Bach: Nineteen Little Preludes*
edited by Christos Tsitsaros

Beach: Gavotte in D minor from *Children's Album*, Op. 36, No. 2
MacDowell: To a Wild Rosef rom *Woodland Sketches*, Op. 51, No. 1
from *The Romantic Era: Intermediate Level*
edited by Richard Walters

German Dance in C Major, WoO 8, No. 7
from *Beethoven: Selected Piano Works*
edited by Matthew Edwards

Restlessness (Inquiétude)
from *Burgmüller: 25 Progressive Studies, Op. 100*
edited by Margaret Otwell

Prelude in A Major, Op. 28, No. 7
from *Chopin: Preludes*
edited by Brian Ganz

Handel: Prelude in G Major from *Suites de pièces*, Volume 2, HWV 442, No. 9
D. Scarlatti: Sonata in D minor, L. 423 (K. 32, P. 14)
from *The Baroque Era: Intermediate Level*
edited by Richard Walters

Study in A minor ("The Avalanche")
from *Heller: Selected Studies, Op. 45 and Op. 46*
edited by William Westney

Lyric Piece
The Chase
from *Kabalevsky: 30 Pieces for Children, Op. 27*
edited by Richard Walters

Andantino
from *Khachaturian: Children's Album, Book 1*
edited by Richard Walters

Funeral March for Signor Maestro Contrapunto, K. 453a
Adagio for Glass Harmonica, K. 356 (617a)
from *Mozart: 15 Intermediate Pieces*
edited by Elena Abend

Morning
Promenade
from *Prokofiev: Music for Children, Op. 65*
edited by Matthew Edwards

Of Strange Lands and People
(Von fremden Ländern und Menschen)
from *Schumann: Scenes from Childhood (Kinderscenen)*, Op. 15
edited by Jeffrey Biegel

Birthday
from *Shostakovich: Children's Notebook for Piano, Op. 69*
edited by Richard Walters

Sonata in D minor

Domenico Scarlatti
L. 423 (K. 32, P. 14)

Fingerings, tempo, articulations, and dynamics are editorial suggestions.
Ornaments have been realized for this edition.

Funeral March for Signor Maestro Contrapunto

Wolfgang Amadeus Mozart
K. 453a

Fingerings are editorial suggestions.

Gavotte in D minor

from *Children's Album*

Amy Marcy Beach
Op. 36, No. 2

Fingerings are from the first edition.

25
p
cresc.
30
p
36
dim.
sopra
poco rit.
pp
41
[a tempo]
pp
47
cresc.
f
52
mf
rit.
f

Andantino

from *Children's Album*, Book 1

Aram Khachaturian

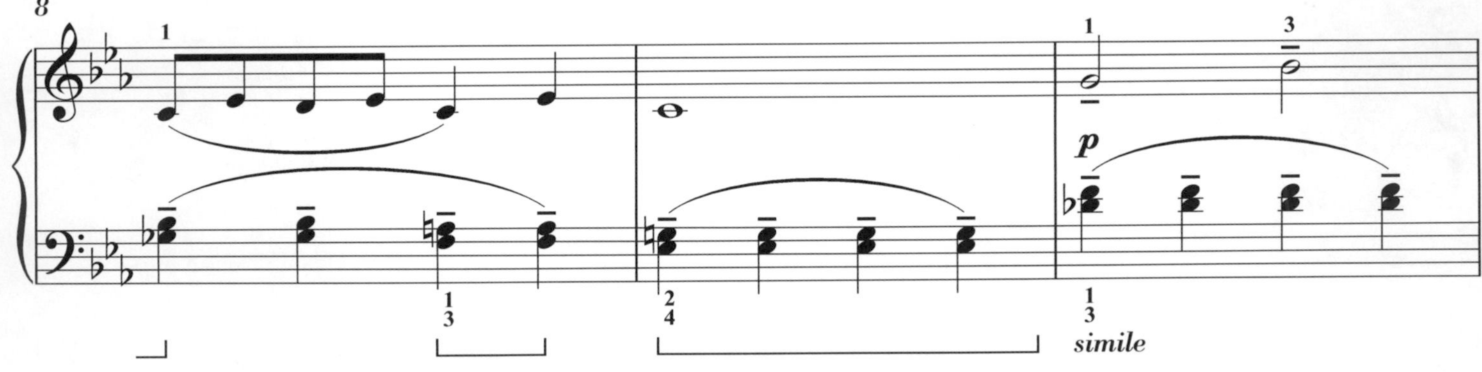

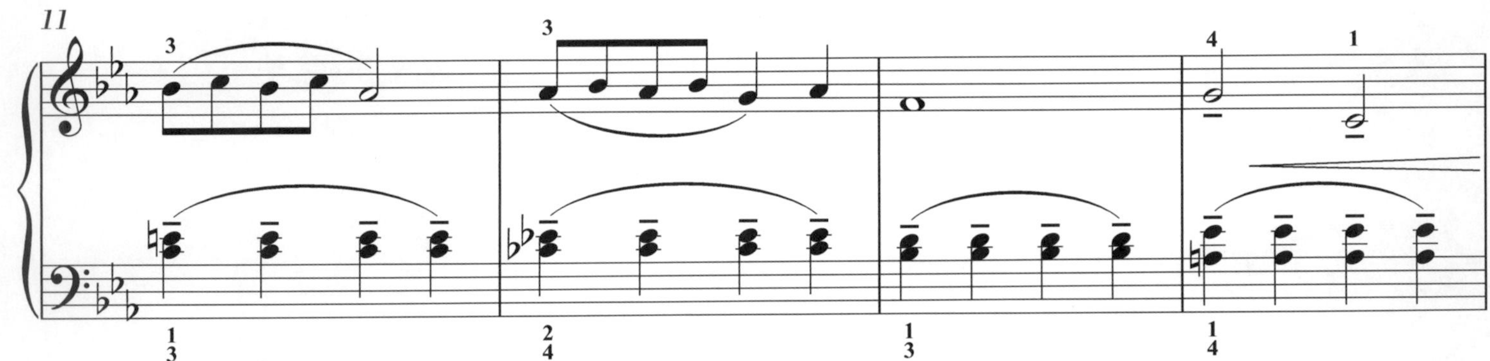

Fingerings are by the composer.

rit.
mf legato
a tempo
f
p

German Dance in C Major

Ludwig van Beethoven
WoO 8, No. 7

Fingerings are editorial suggestions.

(16) Trio

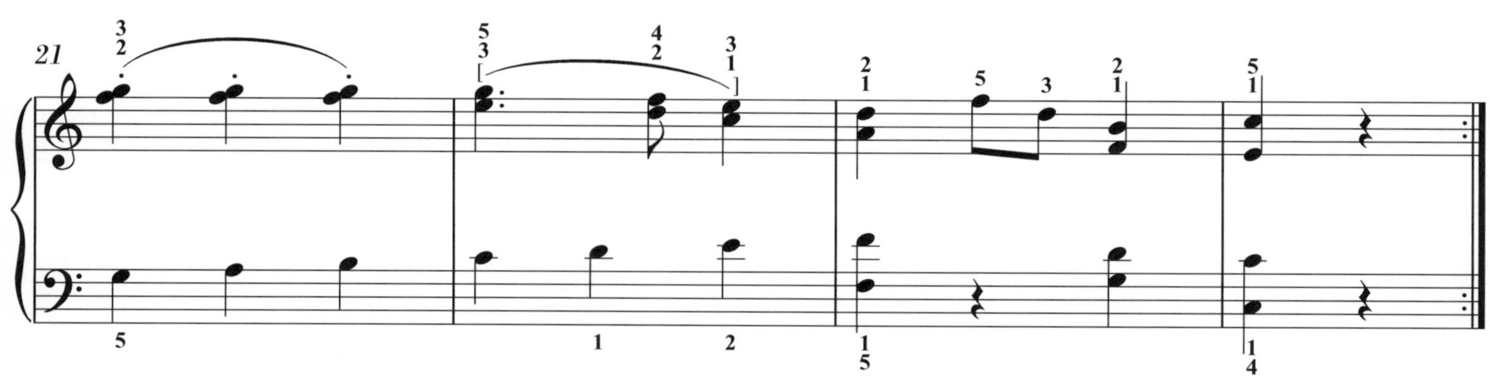
21

(24)

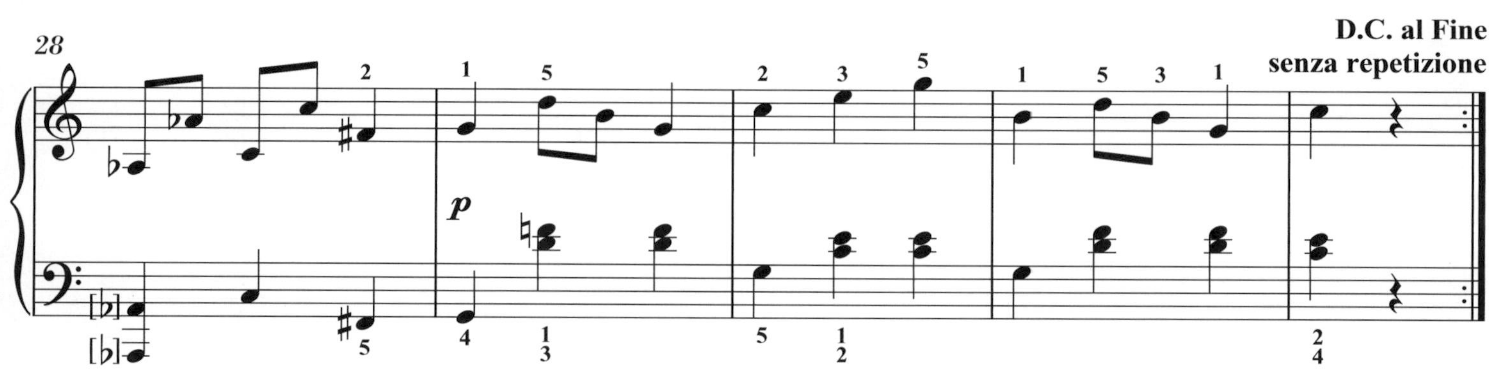
28
D.C. al Fine
senza repetizione

To a Wild Rose

from *Woodland Sketches*

Edward MacDowell
Op. 51, No. 1

Fingerings are editorial suggestions.

still increase
f
diminish
rit.
p [a tempo]
p
mp
slightly marked
p
pp
ppp

Prelude in G Major

from *Suites de pièces*, Volume 2

George Frideric Handel

HWV 442, No. 9

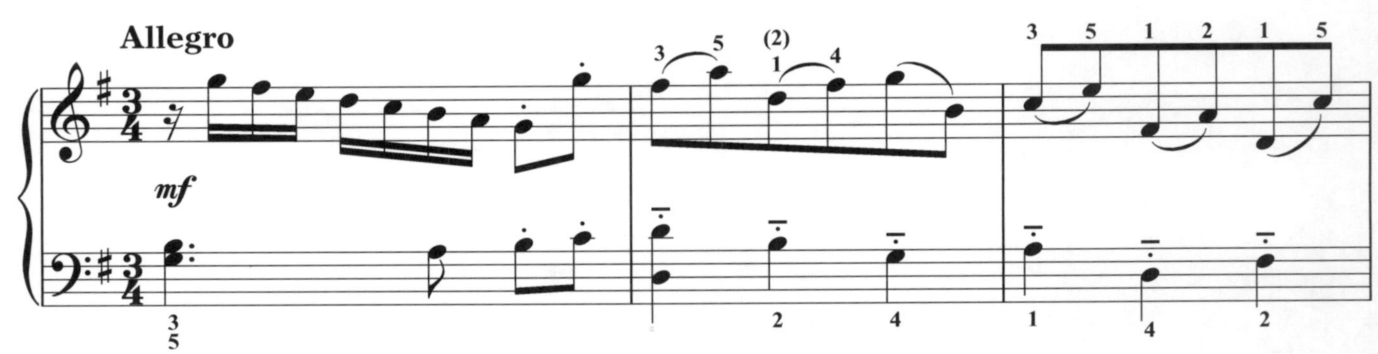

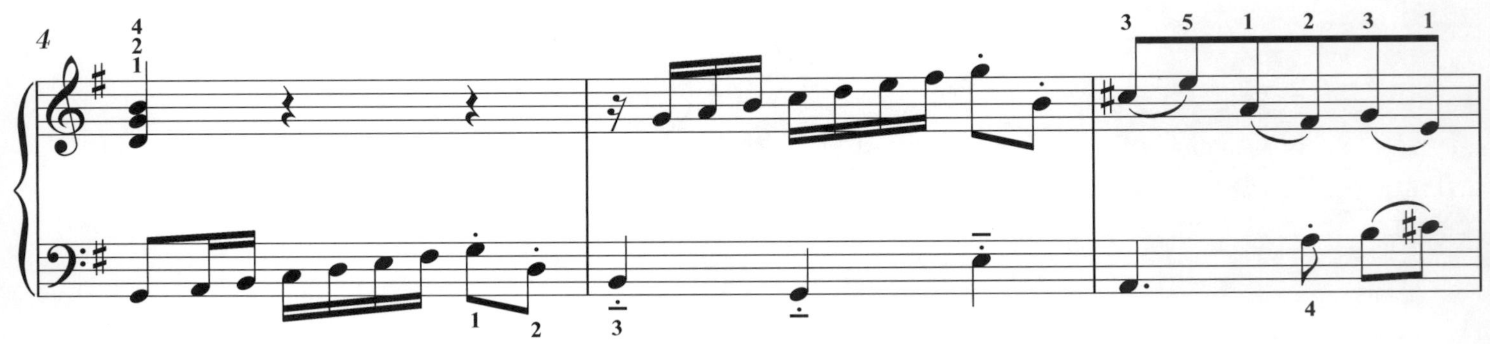

Fingerings, articulations, and dynamics are editorial suggestions.

rit. 2nd time
1.
2.

Restlessness

(Inquiétude)
from *25 Easy and Progressive Studies*

Johann Friedrich Burgmüller
Op. 100, No. 18

Fingerings are editorial suggestions.

16
p a tempo

20
cresc.

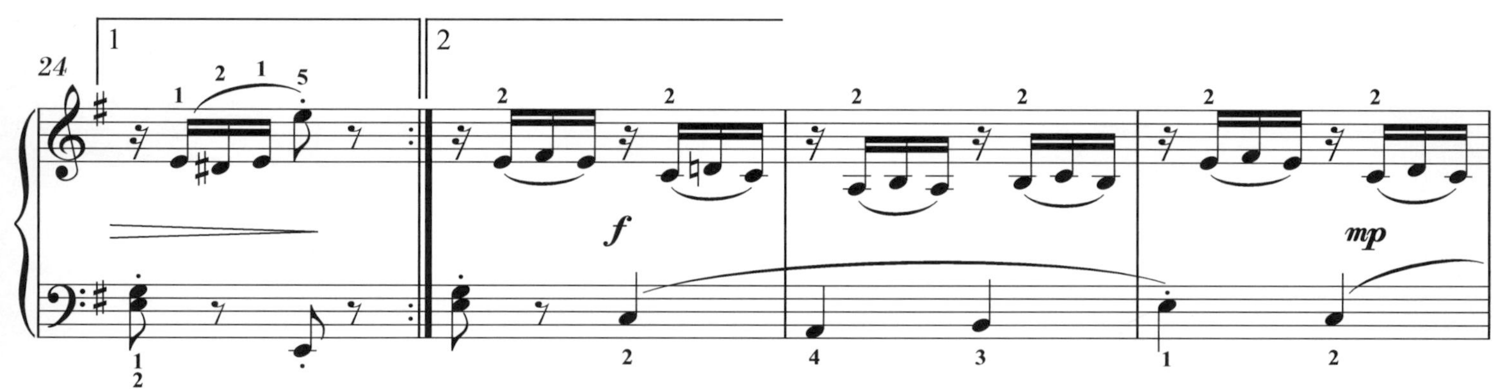
24
1
2
f
mp

28
dim.
p

Adagio for Glass Harmonica

Wolfgang Amadeus Mozart
K. 356 (617a)

Fingerings are editorial suggestions.

[poco rit.]
p
sf
[a tempo]
p

Study in A minor
("The Avalanche")
from *25 Melodious Etudes*

Stephen Heller
Op. 45, No. 2

Fingerings are editorial suggestions.

a tempo
mf
p
cresc.
f
mf
fp
risoluto
8va
sf

The Chase

from *30 Pieces for Children*

Dmitri Kabalevsky
Op. 27, No. 21

Allegro moderato [𝅗𝅥 = c. 96]

Fingerings are editorial suggestions.

mf
cresc.
f
più f
poco rit.
ff

Of Strange Lands and People

(Von fremden Ländern und Menschen)
from *Scenes from Childhood*
(Kinderszenen)

Robert Schumann
Op. 15, No. 1

Fingerings are editorial suggestions.

Birthday

from *Children's Notebook for Piano*

Dmitri Shostakovich
Op. 69, No. 7

Fingerings are editorial suggestions.

mf
f
fff

Tempo I

für mein nur Einziger Böski

Little Shimmy

George Antheil

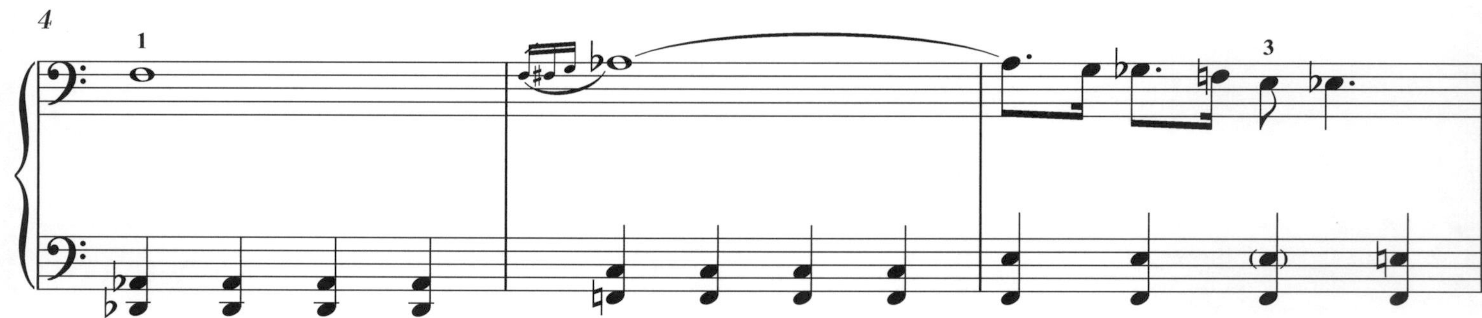

Fingerings are editorial suggestions.

13
16
[p]
19
[mf]
22
25
[p]

Lyric Piece

from *30 Pieces for Children*

Dmitri Kabalevsky
Op. 27, No. 16

Fingerings are editorial suggestions.

ritenuto

Rustic Dance
from *Five Little Dances*

Paul Creston
Op. 24, No. 1

Fingerings are editorial suggestions.

pp
increase
f
ff

to Number 220601

To My Steinway

from *Three Sketches for Pianoforte*

Samuel Barber

Fingerings are editorial suggestions.

Prelude in A Major

Frédéric Chopin
Op. 28, No. 7

Fingerings are editorial suggestions.

to Jean

Petite Berceuse

Samuel Barber

The fingerings in italics are Barber's; all others are editorial suggestions.
Pedaling is editorial suggestion.

8va
accel.
(8va)
Tempo I
sempre pp
dim.

Morning

from *Music for Children*

Sergei Prokofiev
Op. 65, No. 1

Fingerings are editorial suggestions.

pp dolce
p
cantabile
mp
poco cresc.
mf
pochis. rit.
dim.
a tempo
p
mf
mp
dolce
p
pp

à Mademoiselle Jeanne Leleu

Prélude

Maurice Ravel

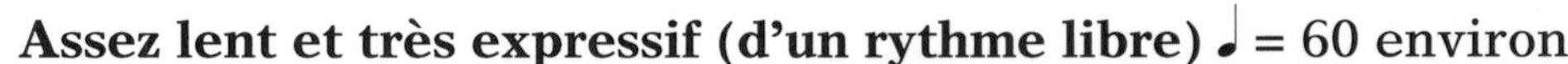

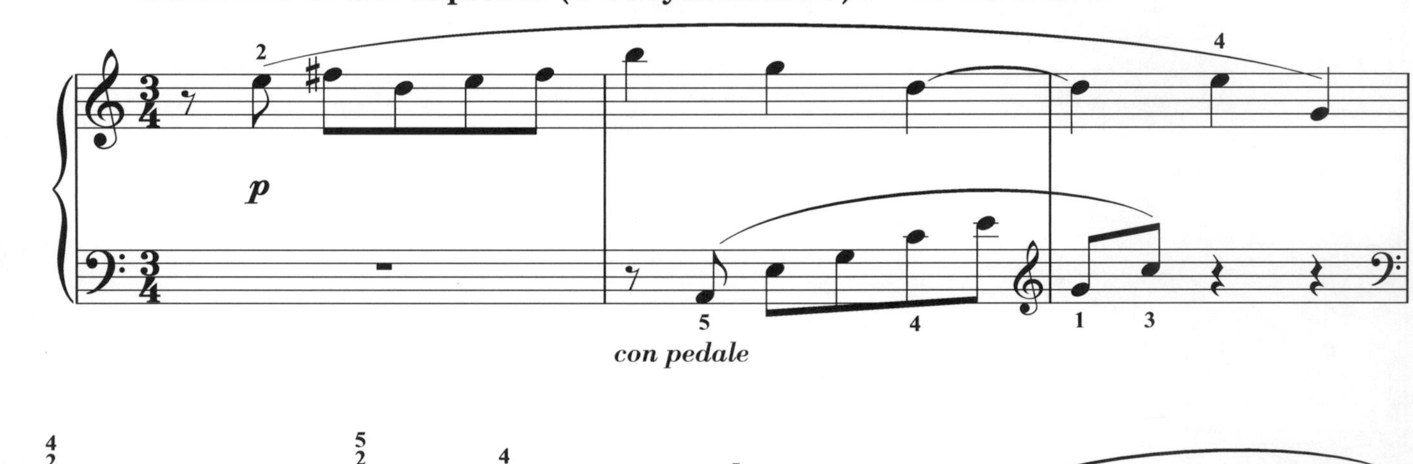

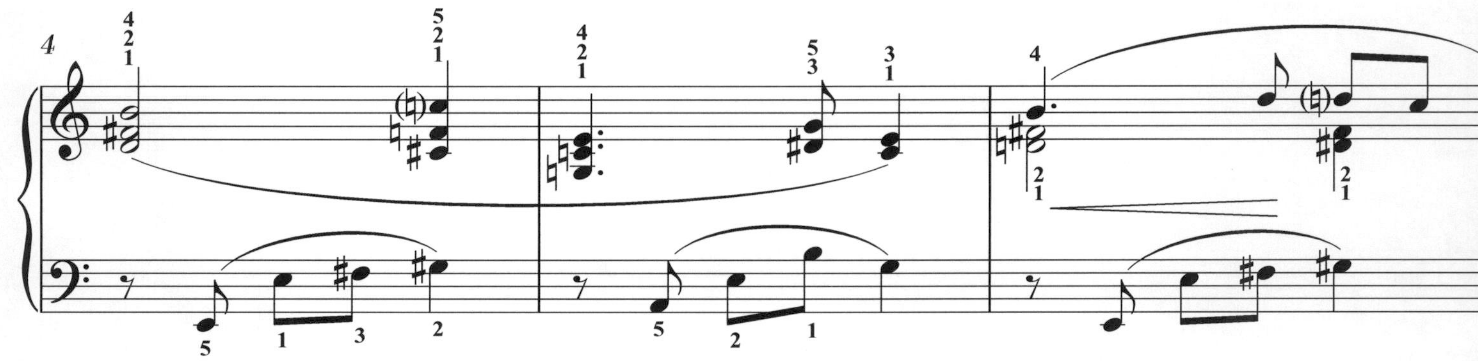

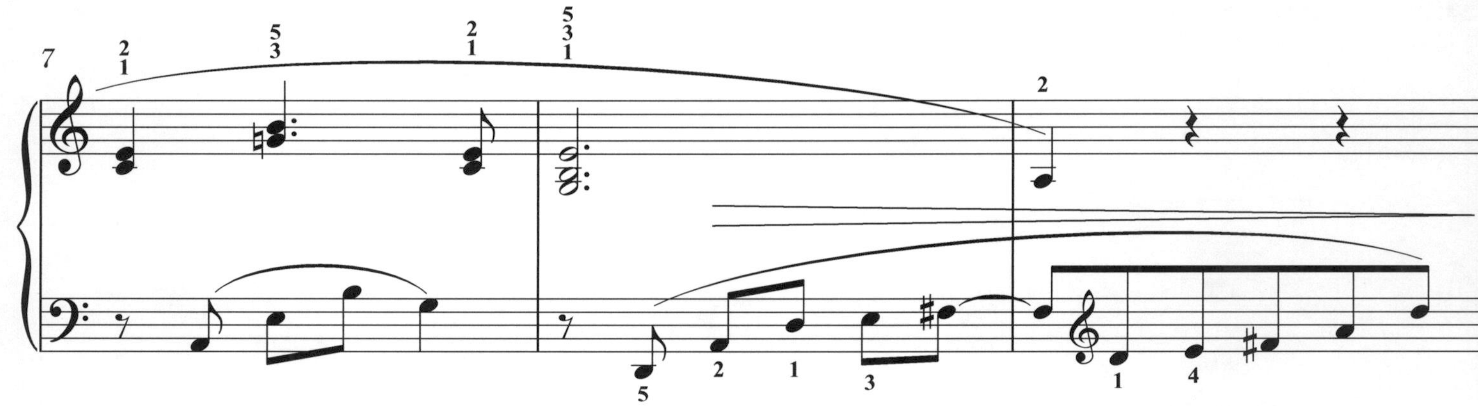

Fingerings are editorial suggestions.

Ralenti
au Mouvt
p
L.H. over
con pedale
Ralenti
Très lent
pp
L.H. over

Prelude in C minor

Johann Sebastian Bach
BWV 999

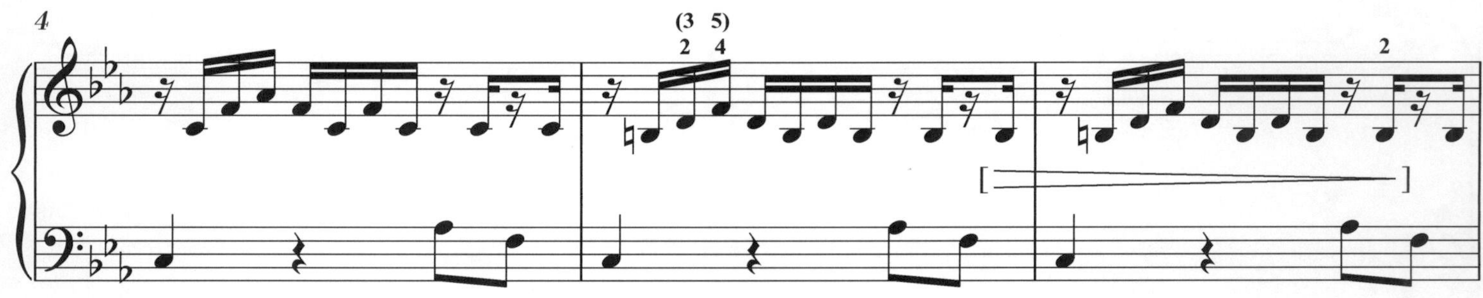

Fingerings are editorial suggestions.

13
(3 5 3 2)
2 4 2 1
5
1 3
(2)
(3 5)
2 4
[
2 3
2 5
mf]
5
1 2
16
3 5
[
4
1 2
2 4
mp]
1 2
19
2 5
[poco a poco cresc.]
1 2
3 5
1 2
(5)
3 4
1 2
22
2 5
1 2
3 5
[f]
1 2
2 5
1 2
25
3 5
1 2
2 5
2 4
1 3

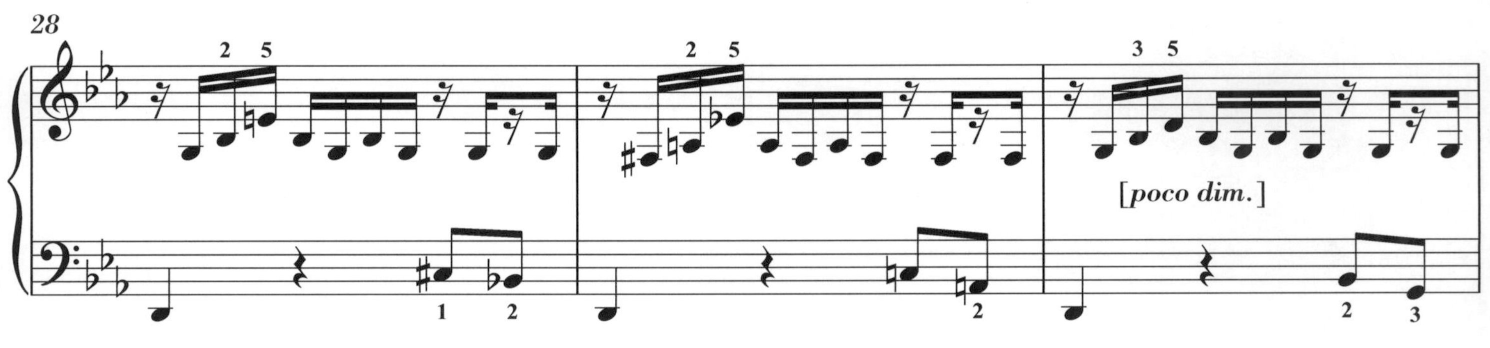
28
[poco dim.]

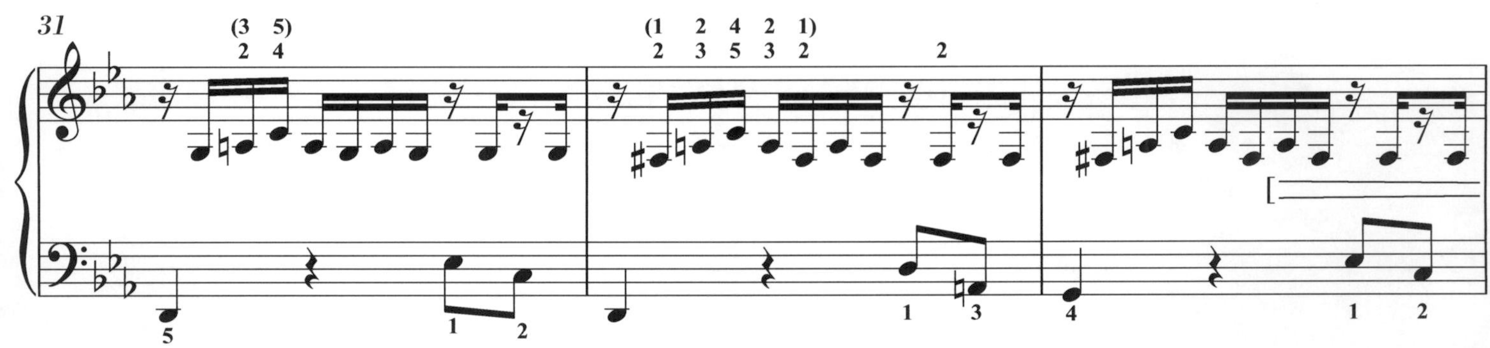
31

34
p]
[poco cresc.]

37
[mf]
[poco dim.]

40
f]

Solfeggietto in C minor

Carl Philipp Emanuel Bach
H. 220

Fingerings and dynamics are editorial suggestions.

10
[f]
12
14
[p]
[f]
16
[p]
[f]
18

21
2
1
2
3
[p]

24
[f]
[p]

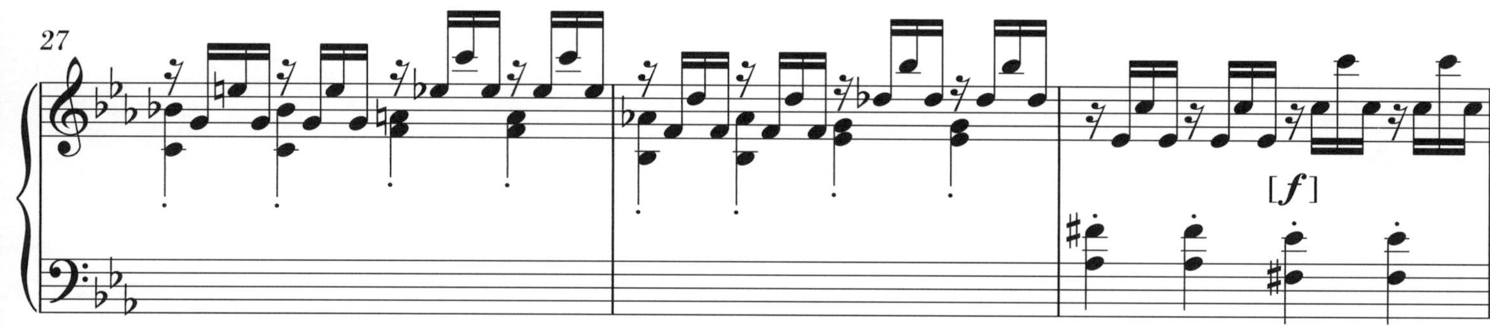
27
[f]

30
[p]

33

Frère Jacques

from *Scènes enfantines*

Mélanie Bonis
Op. 92, No. 6

Fingerings are by the composer.

cresc.
mf
dim.
p
crescendo
f
Un peu plus lent
tres court
dim.
mp
p
dim.
ppp
8vb

Prelude in D minor

Johann Sebastian Bach
BWV 926

Fingerings are editorial suggestions.

27
[mp]
[cresc.]
32
37
[f]
r.h.
l.h.
41
ossia
44
(e)
[mf] [rit.]
(f)
(e)
(f)

Fable No. 9
from *Fables*

Robert Muczynski
Op. 21, No. 9

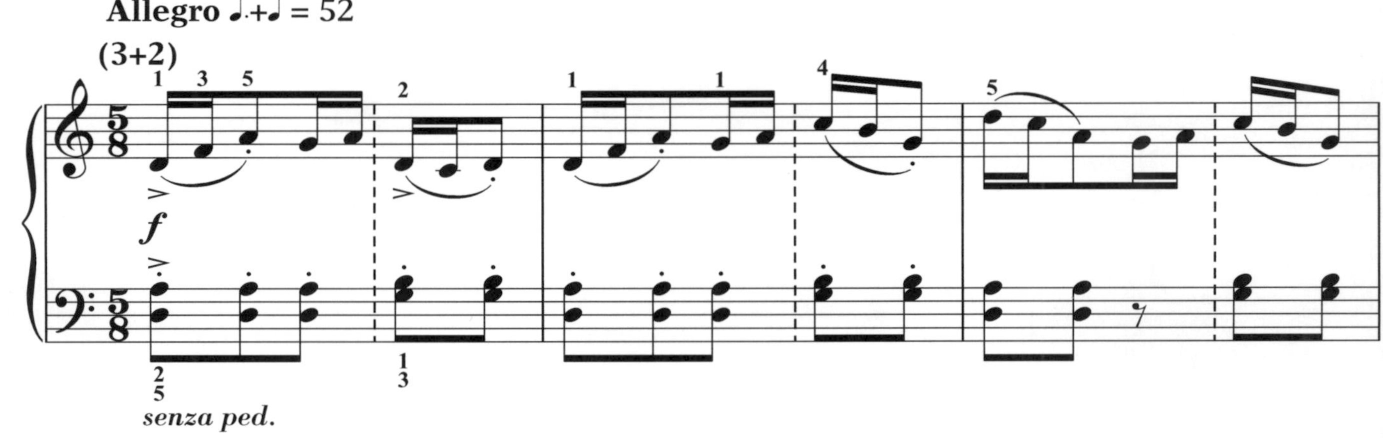

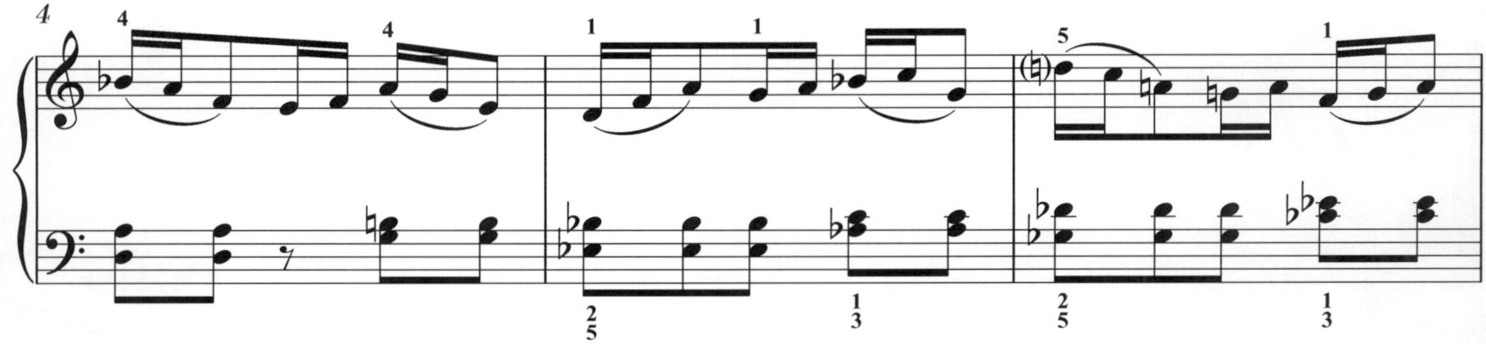

Fingerings are editorial suggestions.

mf
p
sub. f
allarg.
ff

Promenade

from *Music for Children*

Sergei Prokofiev
Op. 65, No. 2

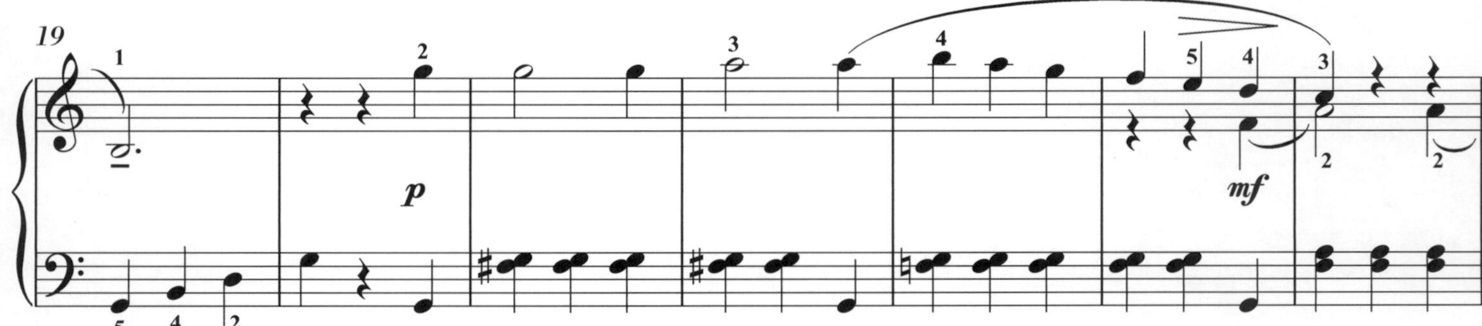

Fingerings are editorial suggestions.

mf
p
mf
p
mf
p
mf
dim.
p
dolce
mp
p

Rondo-Toccata

from *Four Rondos*

Dmitri Kabalevsky
Op. 60, No. 4

Fingerings are by the composer.

26
31
mp
36
41
47
f
marcato

mp